CW00621804

Keep this pocket-sized Fri
you are visiting Mancheste
in the locality.

Whether you are in your car or on foot, you will
enjoy an evocative journey back in time. Compare
the Manchester of old with what you can see
today—see how the streets of the city and its parks
and open spaces have changed; examine the shops
and buildings and notice how they have been altered
or replaced; look at fine details such as lamp-posts,
shop fascias and trade signs; and see the many
alterations to Manchester and its surrounding
villages that have taken place unnoticed during our
lives, some of which we may have taken for granted.

At the turn of a page you will gain fascinating
insights into Manchester's unique history.

FRANCIS / FRITH'S
pocket ALBUM

MANCHESTER

A POCKET ALBUM

Adapted from an original book by
CLIFF HAYES

First published in the United Kingdom in 2004 by
Frith Book Company Ltd

ISBN 1-85937-883-8

British Library Cataloguing in Publication Data

Manchester—A Pocket Album
Adapted from an original book by Cliff Hayes

Frith Book Company Ltd
Frith's Barn, Teffont,
Salisbury, Wiltshire SP3 5QP
Tel: +44 (0) 1722 716 376
Email: info@francisfrith.co.uk
www.francisfrith.co.uk

Printed and bound in Great Britain by MPG, Bodmin

Front Cover: **MANCHESTER, MARKET STREET** 1889 21899
The colour-tinting is for illustrative purposes only, and is not intended to be historically accurate.

Frontispiece: **MANCHESTER, PICCADILLY** 1895 36383

CONTENTS

FRANCIS FRITH
VICTORIAN PIONEER

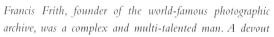

Francis Frith, founder of the world-famous photographic archive, was a complex and multi-talented man. A devout Quaker and a highly successful Victorian businessman, he was philosophic by nature and pioneering in outlook. By 1855 he had already established a wholesale grocery business in Liverpool, and sold it for the astonishing sum of £200,000, which is the equivalent today of over £15,000,000. Now in his thirties, and captivated by the new science of photography, Frith set out on a series of pioneering journeys up the Nile and to the Near East.

INTRIGUE AND EXPLORATION

He was the first photographer to venture beyond the sixth cataract of the Nile. Africa was still the mysterious 'Dark Continent', and Stanley and Livingstone's historic meeting was a decade into the future. The conditions for picture taking confound belief. He laboured for hours in his wicker dark-room in the sweltering heat of the desert, while the volatile chemicals fizzed dangerously in their trays. Back in London he exhibited his photographs and was 'rapturously cheered' by members of the Royal Society. His reputation as a photographer was made overnight.

VENTURE OF A LIFE-TIME

By the 1870s the railways had threaded their way across the country, and Bank Holidays and half-day Saturdays had been made obligatory by Act of Parliament. All of a sudden the working man and his family were able to enjoy days out, take holidays, and see a little more of the world.

With typical business acumen, Francis Frith foresaw that these new tourists would enjoy having souvenirs to commemorate their days out. For the next thirty years he travelled the country by train and by pony and trap, producing fine photographs of seaside resorts and beauty spots that were keenly bought by millions of Victorians. These prints were painstakingly pasted into family albums and pored over during the dark nights of winter, rekindling precious memories of summer excursions. Frith's studio was soon supplying retail shops all over the country, and by 1890 F Frith & Co had become the greatest specialist photographic publishing company in the world, with over 2,000 sales outlets, and pioneered the picture postcard.

FRANCIS FRITH'S LEGACY

Francis Frith had died in 1898 at his villa in Cannes, his great project still growing. The archive he created continued in business for another seventy years. By 1970 it contained over a third of a million pictures showing 7,000 British towns and villages.

Frith's legacy to us today is of immense significance and value, for the magnificent archive of evocative photographs he created provides a unique record of change in the cities, towns and villages throughout Britain over a century and more. Frith and his fellow studio photographers revisited locations many times down the years to update their views, compiling for us an enthralling and colourful pageant of British life and character.

We are fortunate that Frith was dedicated to recording the minutiae of everyday life. For it is this sheer wealth of visual data, the painstaking chronicle of changes in dress, transport, street layouts, buildings, housing, engineering and landscape that captivates us so much today, offering us a powerful link with the past and with the lives of our ancestors.

Computers have now made it possible for Frith's many thousands of images to be accessed almost instantly. The archive offers every one of us an opportunity to examine the places where we and our families have lived and worked down the years. Its images, depicting our shared past, are now bringing pleasure and enlightenment to millions around the world a century and more after his death.

MANCHESTER, THE CATHEDRAL 1897 39042

MANCHESTER
AN INTRODUCTION

'THE FASTEST GROWING town in England', was how Manchester was described two hundred and fifty years ago. There seemed to be a determination in the minds of the burghers and leading citizens to make something of the place, to push forward this small town in north-west England and stamp its name not just on the rest of the country, but on the world. They succeeded, and in the years that followed Manchester became the place where the first canal system was started, passenger railways were born, and plans for a great ship canal were hatched - and in more recent times, it was the birth-place of the modern computer.

Manchester has never been frightened to take in the stranger, the foreigner or the outsider. It was this willingness that brought the Flemish weavers here in around 1363; Colonel John Rosworm, a German, defended the town during the Civil War in the 17th century; and Karl Marx and Frederick Engels - and the Rothchilds - came here in the 19th century.

Manchester had to break away from the strong influence of Salford, which *ruled over the ancient 'hundred' and which seemed to hold all the power in the area for a long time. Manchester's influence increased by the fact that the parish church was situated in Manchester; after it was turned into a Collegiate Church, Manchester became the centre of learning and law-making in the area. It was weaving, first of woollen goods, then of cotton, which brought Manchester its power and its glory. Because people like Humphrey Chetham gave fair wages and dealt honestly in the newly-emerging cotton industry, Manchester advanced by leaps and bounds.*

The Charter of Incorporation of the Borough of Manchester was granted by Queen Victoria on 23 October 1838. There had been some unrest at the way Manchester had been managed, and it was Richard Cobden who urged Mancunians to 'put an end to this thing' and have a council elected by the people. After the Municipal Corporation Act had been passed in 1835, many Lancashire towns had started down the road to becoming Boroughs, but Manchester did not become a Corporation until that day in 1838; after much debate, and accusations of vote rigging and ballot fixing, Manchester was given the right to set aside the self-elected officials and hold the first municipal election.

The Charter which made Manchester a city was granted on 29 March 1853, so it had risen from a suburb of Salford to a city in only fifteen years. The town's progress to the status of city was rapid, probably the fastest in England. By 1839 it had its own Justice of the Peace, and by 1842 a coat of arms, a crest and motto - 'Concilio et Labore', 'By Council and Work'. The rivalry between Liverpool and Manchester was such that advisers to Queen Victoria said that the honour of the title Lord Mayor could not be given to one city and not the other. At exactly 11am on 3 August 1893, one of Queen Victoria's ministers entered the office of both Liverpool and Manchester's mayors and laid before them her majesty's permission to the title Lord Mayor; thus neither could claim a victory over the other. Since then, Greater Manchester has taken quite a few forms, including that of a new county. The spirit and perseverance of old Manchester still drives it forward.

THE CATHEDRAL 1889 21868

Victoria Street passes in front of the cathedral. We can see a part of the North Porch at the side of the tower. There was still a graveyard on the Fennel Street side, and Chetham's College and courtyard can be seen next door.

THE CATHEDRAL

1899   43334

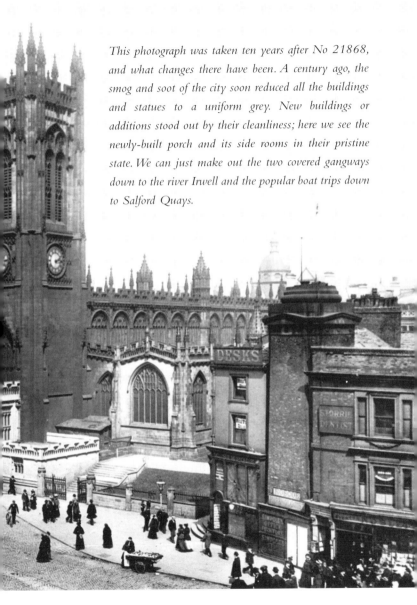

This photograph was taken ten years after No 21868, and what changes there have been. A century ago, the smog and soot of the city soon reduced all the buildings and statues to a uniform grey. New buildings or additions stood out by their cleanliness; here we see the newly-built porch and its side rooms in their pristine state. We can just make out the two covered gangways down to the river Irwell and the popular boat trips down to Salford Quays.

This view looks from Fennel Street, with Cathedral Street going off to the left. This corner of the Cathedral (the Manchester Regiment Chapel) was badly damaged in the blitz of the Second World War. The window that you can see to the left of the lamp-post now has modern stained glass in it, in wonderful reds and oranges, to depict the flames of the bombing; it was designed as a tribute to the Cathedral and to Manchester's rise from that episode. The wall we see on the right and the graveyard behind were cleared away in the 1950s.

THE CATHEDRAL 1897 39042

This view shows how the Cathedral also played the role of a parish church; it was surrounded with the burial stones of the town's faithful. The St Nicholas Chapel was built in 1311 and contains the Trafford family tombs under the floor.

THE CATHEDRAL 1889 21866

The Lady Chapel is behind the high altar; unfortunately, all the lovely stained glass seen here was blown out in December 1940 when the cathedral was bombed. The rebuilding took nearly twenty years, and the craftsmen tried to put only the best and finest materials back into Manchester's chief house of God. 192 new traceried panels were fitted to the ancient beams of the choir roof. Thousands of pieces of new wood had to be let into the elaborate canopies of the choir stalls seen here. Most of these stalls had been put here by Sir James Stanley in 1513. He was brother to the man who married the mother of Henry VII, and the family enjoyed power and influence for centuries later. The Derby Chapel on the left, where he now rests, later became the Manchester Regiment Chapel in 1936, when the then Lord Derby gave it to the Regiment.

THE
CATHEDRAL
CHOIR C1885 18250

15

We are looking at the choir screen and the organ above it from the main body of the church. The choir where the Bishop and church dignitaries sat was beyond the screen, cut off from the congregation. The high screen, with organ pipes topped with pointed angel wings, has been in place for more than 400 years. The organ was one of the very best in the country and technically superb, ranking tenth in Great Britain. It was completely destroyed in the blitz and could not be saved. Note the pulpit on the left

THE CATHEDRAL 1889 21870

HORSE-DRAWN TRAMS,

DEANSGATE 1892 30384

Unusually, both the trams near our camera are facing the same way on adjacent lines. To make the turning round of trams easier, lines were laid right round the Victoria Buildings, seen here on the right, so that trams could circle the building and face outward again. This arrangement lasted until the Second World War.

This view was taken from St Ann's Square. This building is the third Exchange to be built in this area. The first was in the Market Place, near St Ann's Square, built in 1729 at the expense of Sir Oswald Mosley, Lord of the Manor. It was taken down in 1793, and a new Exchange was started in 1806. By 1849 there had been two extensions added, along with a post office and news room. To celebrate these two new extensions a full-dress ball was held, and the money raised went to the Baths and Wash-House Fund. The building we see here (the third) was started in 1867; the first part opened on 2 October 1871, and the building was completed by October 1874.

THE ROYAL EXCHANGE 1886 18259

THE GREAT HALL, THE
ROYAL EXCHANGE 1885 18262

This was dubbed at the time 'the largest room in the world'. It was 4,405 square yards in area, and 96ft high and 125ft high to the top of the central dome. In this huge hall, cotton merchants from all over Lancashire did their bartering, and many a fortune was made or lost. At one stage there were eleven thousand members, who met every Tuesday and Friday to conduct business. There were numbers on the posts running down the hall, and letters on the posts across the hall, so businesses could co-ordinate where to meet in such a busy and packed room.

ST ANN'S SQUARE AND THE
CHURCH 1886 18265

The Royal Exchange dominates Exchange Street, which starts where the square becomes narrower. The statue of John Cobden can been seen in the middle of the square: this bronze statue, by Marshall Wood, was paid for by public subscription and was presented to the town on 23 April 1867 by the President of the Anti-Corn Law League, George Wilson. The buildings on the right were put up around 1835; the one with rounded window arches was for a long time the booksellers Sherratt & Hughes, and later Waterstones - it then became WH Smiths while the Arndale Centre was being rebuilt.

ST ANN'S SQUARE c1876 8290

*Hansom cabs await customers.
Because the square was the
home of many businesses, the
rank would usually be a busy
place, with customers coming
and going. Many businesses took
lunch and closed at 12 noon till
2.30pm or even up to 4.00pm,
but they did start at 7.00am and
often did not close till 8.00pm
or later. Our photograph is
taken almost from the church
door, and the area nearest the
camera was once the graveyard.
As you walk the area today, it
is hard to imagine how many
souls rest under the concrete
and paving stones. Manchester's
first election for MPs was held
in the square, and after a day
of speech-making Philips and
Poulett were duly elected.*

CAB RANK

ST ANN'S SQUARE 1885 18263

This view looks from the top of King Street down towards Cross Street. We can see that the street narrows towards the bottom. This part of the street was going to be called St James's Square, a challenge by the Roman Catholic, originally Stuart-supporting element, to St Ann's Square, which was named for a Church of England Queen. The third building away from the camera on the right was Manchester's first Town Hall, started in 1825; it was the centre of municipal administration until the new town hall opened in 1877.

KING STREET c1885 18287

Corporation Street was the last major roadway development in the city centre made by the corporation. Before it was cut and constructed in the 1870s, traffic from the north-west and higher Salford had to wend its way through small back streets to reach the market and central Manchester (the Shambles).

CORPORATION STREET
C1885   18276

This street was once called Market Stead Lane, and led from the newly-emerging warehouses around Piccadilly to the Market Place, Acres Field and the Shambles. Before it was widened, Market Street was a narrow, crooked and steeply-rising lane; in places it was so narrow that only one cart could pass at a time. Things became so bad that an Act to improve Market Street was passed in 1821. The buildings we see here were constructed around 1850, and the street became the main shopping area for Manchester

MARKET STREET 1889 21899

MARKET STREET 1886 18270

This is the top of Market Street, adjacent to Piccadilly. Lewis's building is on the left, and Rylands Store is opposite on the right: two of the most successful princes of commerce, and two great influences on the way we shop today, are facing each other at the top of Manchester's most commercial retail thoroughfare. The Rylands building was rebuilt at the turn of the century, and the building went on to be Paulden's Store and today Debenhams. Marks & Spencer's first large shop was in this building. 'Good & Cheap' is one of the slogans outside Rylands.

LEWIS'S BUILDING,
MARKET STREET 1889 21900

We are looking from the Cross Street / Corporation Street corner. The art of bartering was just dying out. Fifty years before, you would spend a long time on every purchase discussing the price and making offers. David Lewis had advertised that 'our prices are the lowest possible and NO deviation from the marked price will be made'; the public took to the system, much to the amazement of the other shops. Note the third shop on the left, Brooke Bond & Co: this was a Manchester firm of tea and coffee importers founded by Samuel Brooke.

MARKET STREET 1889 21914

TRAFFIC IN
MARKET STREET
C1885 18266

The City Art Gallery building was started in 1825 and completed in 1830 at a cost of £30,000. Designed in Grecian style and proportions by Sir Charles Barry, who also designed the Houses of Parliament, it was built as a home for the Royal Institution of Manchester. The Corporation were given the building on the understanding that they spent £2,000 per year buying works of art. Among its treasures were copies of the Elgin Marbles, presented by George IV, and a statue of John Dalton in marble. As an Art Gallery there was never enough space, and many works of art have had to be stored away. The year 2000 saw the gallery closed while work began on expanding it to take in new buildings, including the Athenaeum Club next door on Princess Street.

THE ART GALLERY AND MOSLEY STREET 1885 1828s

Mosley Street was named in honour of Sir Nicholas Mosley, a former Lord of the Manor of Manchester. The other fine buildings along the street include the Portico Library and St Peter's Church. The art gallery was one of the first supporters of the local artist L S Lowry, and has a wonderful collection of his work.

THE ART GALLERY c1885 18286

THE VICTORIA
BUILDINGS 1889 21898

The Victoria Buildings were built in the late 1880s and named in honour of Queen Victoria's fifty years on the throne. This building, that dominated the cathedral end of Deansgate, included twenty-eight shops, eighty-eight offices and forty-eight cellars, as well as a two hundred and thirty-one roomed hotel. Our view is from the Royal Exchange Building. St Mary's Gate is to the left, and the now lost Victoria Street is away to the right, leading to Exchange Station; Cromwell's Statue can just be seen on the far right.

We are looking from the second floor of the Victoria Hotel. Manchester Exchange Station (technically in Salford) is on the left, the Cathedral on the right. The approach to the station is a bridge over the River Irwell. At the centre bottom of our picture is Cromwell's statue, by Alfred Noble. This was conceived by Thomas Goadsby, though it was presented to the city by Mrs Abel Heywood; this was her second marriage - Thomas Goadsby was her first husband, and it was Thomas Goadsby who commissioned and paid for the statue. She wanted it here on the banks of the Irwell because Thomas had saved her life here when her father's boat, the 'Emma', capsized on its launch. Many people were drowned in the tragedy. Oliver Cromwell's statue is now in Wythenshawe Park, minus his sword.

VIEW FROM
VICTORIA
HOTEL 1889   2 1884

37

Victoria Buildings was more than just a hotel. Insurance companies had offices here, and there were shops too. Here we see one of the ornate gateways that gave entrance to the inner square of the building for deliveries. There were cellars for rent, and Manchester businesses could store goods in them. The power for the lifts was provided by a hydraulic water-power system that came directly from the pump house situated on Quay Street, by the River Irwell, where the water came from.

THE GATEWAY TO VICTORIA
BUILDINGS c1873 8288

This view was taken from Oxford Street Corner. This street was known as the street of warehouses. Only fifty years earlier, this street had been nothing more than a dirt track with some third-rate shops. The warehouses started transforming the street about 1845, and the businesses we can see here include A & S Henry (Importers), the famous S & J Watts & Co, and Sam Mendel, a rope and twine manufacturer, who lived at Manley Park, Chorlton.

PORTLAND STREET 1885 18284

We are looking up Aytoun Street towards Piccadilly, with the dome of the Infirmary building in the square, and the Grand Hotel building dominating the right of the photograph. We can tell from the squareness of this building that the Grand Hotel started life as a warehouse in 1867. In 1880 it was converted to an hotel, and it remained an hotel for almost a hundred years. Today, in the year 2000, it has just re-opened as rather grand high-tech service flats. Aytoun Street gets its name from Roger Aytoun (known as Spanking Roger), who came to Manchester from Scotland as an officer in the army. He married a local lady of means, Barbara Minshull, and spent the next ten years going through her considerable fortune.

THE GRAND HOTEL C1885 18290

PICCADILLY 1889 22158

The area from the Duke of Wellington statue to Market Street was once a large ornamental pond complete with fountains, which had delighted Queen Victoria and Prince Albert on their visit in 1840. Before that, the area was called the 'dawb holes'; clay was taken from here to make local bricks. At the time of our picture, it was newly laid out and paved.

THE ROYAL INFIRMARY
C1885 18256

The Royal Infirmary, with its high dome and clock face, lords it over Piccadilly. The hospital opened in 1775; the portico entrance nearest the camera was the front of a Mental Asylum, which was incorporated into the building. A public bath house was also part of the block; as well as serving the people of the back streets around Piccadilly, it meant that patients could be given a bath before entering hospital. The cabs in the picture include the famous hansom cab, designed and built by Charles Hansom of Manchester.

The dome of the Infirmary is on the left, and Lewis's tower is in the centre. On Tuesday 1 September 1908, a large crowd gathered here to watch about one hundred patients being moved out of the Infirmary. Horse-drawn ambulances, taxi cabs, flat wagons, and even a horse bus were used to convey the patients down to the new Royal Infirmary on Oxford Road. Only one patient was left behind because he was too ill to move. The main buildings were soon demolished, but the Wash House remained, as did part of the Asylum, which was used as a reference library before the Central Library was built.

PICCADILLY 1895 36382

THE PUBLIC GARDENS,
PICCADILLY c1965 M21051

This is a central and popular spot for shoppers and office workers to sit and relax in the well-laid-out formal gardens. There have been more plans for this area of open space than there are hot sunny days in the average summer. The area was going to be an art gallery, a town hall extension, an hotel, and an entertainment complex - but none of these plans came to fruition. Underneath Piccadilly were built rooms from where the area could be controlled if the Russians started a war. There were cardboard coffins, condensed milk, and other emergency supplies in case the Cold War ever came to the boil.

This is the corner of Piccadilly, where it meets the top of Market Street. On the left is one of Lewis's entrances. Pauldens, in the centre, moved here after a fire destroyed their store in 1957. Part of the newly-laid-out Piccadilly Bus Station can be seen here, looking very clean and neat. Today, this area is dominated by the new tram system, and this end of the bus station has disappeared altogether.

MARKET STREET AND
PICCADILLY JUNCTION c1965 M21046

*These are the premises of the bank run as Cunliffe Brooks & Co, one of Manchester's
private banks. Chancery Lane is to the left of the building, and Brown Street runs
away to the right. The whole building was put up by the Bank of England in 1826,
its second branch in the provinces. Samuel Brooks bought the premises in 1847
when the Bank of England moved out to newer premises. The Bank of England
entrance was on King Street, so Mr Brooks constructed this entrance, complete with
its wonderful crown, to establish his bank in Manchester.*

BROOKS' BANK c1873 8289

This was how the Town Hall in Albert Square looked twelve years after its official opening in 1877. The area at the front of the town hall had been cleared in about 1862 to make space for a memorial to 'Albert the Good', the beloved husband of Queen Victoria. It was a densely built-up area. Albert Square adjoined the Town Yard, land that the corporation owned, and which was already being viewed as a site for a new Town Hall. Princess Street, to the left, was originally called Prince's Street, after Queen Victoria's sons.

THE TOWN HALL 1889 21896

Although Alfred Waterhouse's Town Hall dominates the scene, it is the small round building almost in the middle of our picture that intrigues me. I am told that it was a 'Pistourie', or gentlemen's convenience, and a copy of what was all the rage in Paris at the time. It had been amended from the original to cover gentlemen right to the floor. Thus Manchester's first public convenience, right in the middle of Albert Square, was also a truly fashionable one!

ALBERT SQUARE AND THE TOWN HALL 1889 21894

THE TOWN
HALL 1895 36380

This view was taken from Cross Street corner. Princess Street is running away to the left, with the big bay window on the corner of the building. That room was the mayor's personal receiving room, and the windows meant that a watch could be kept for anyone important approaching the Town Hall. What we cannot see until we are inside is the light airiness of the building: there is a lot of light coming from the triangular open spaces in the middle, and from above. When the Town Hall opened, it also contained a police station complete with cells. By 1895 there were three statues in Albert Square as well as the Albert Memorial.

THE TOWN HALL 1895 36381

The marble statue of John Bright, by A Bruce Joy, was unveiled in Albert Square on 12 October 1891 by Lord Derby. John Bright, with his close associate Cobden, was a passionate believer in free trade. His gift of oratory enabled him to delivery moving speeches with sincerity and passion. He worked tirelessly for the repeal of the Corn Laws, which came about in 1846. John Bright was elected MP for Manchester in 1847, but his outspoken opposition to the Crimean War and his Quaker moral sense of duty turned Manchester people against him. When he stood as MP for Manchester in 1857 he was rejected, and an effigy of him was burnt in the stree

JOHN BRIGHT 1892 30383

CHETHAM ROOM,
CHETHAM COLLEGE 1889 22258

The name Humphrey Chetham and his charitable work is synonymous with Manchester's history. When he died in 1653, Humphrey Chetham had already started the work of educating the 'sons of honest, industrious and painful parents'. His will left money to make sure that the work continued, and it was August 1656 before Chetham's College opened. Here we see the Audit room, with its 15th-century ceiling and fine plasterwork, and panelling from the 1500s.

This is the reading room of Chetham's library. The wonderful thing is that it looks exactly the same today. The long case clock was the first thing given to the college by an ex-pupil, Nicholas Clegg, who presented it to the College in 1695. He made a barometer on the front himself. This room has been a favourite of many famous people. It was in this room that Marx and Engels spent many hours philosophising on the class struggle, and discussing economic and political theories.

CHETHAM COLLEGE
HUMPHREY CHETHAMS ROOM 1889 22259

'The Oldest Licensed House in Great Britain', claimed the sign, 'Licensed over 540 years'. This is very hard to prove, as early licences were issued very haphazardly, and for different reasons. It was said that this old inn had many tunnels radiating from its cellars, and that Guy Fawkes once hid in them. Unfortunately, this lovely old building was pulled down and cleared away as recently as the 1930s.

THE SEVEN STARS INN
C1900 M21301

This gothic pile on Great Ducie Street was opened on 26 July 1864, when Manchester held its first Assize Session here. The Strangeway Estate had been bought around 1859 for the purpose of building a gaol and these courts. Alfred Waterhouse, who designed Manchester's Town Hall, was given the job of providing a court building to match the city's growing importance. It was once said that Waterhouse had designed for all classes of Mancunians.

THE ASSIZE COURT 1886 1825l

The church's foundation stone was laid on 11 December 1788, and the church was consecrated on 6 September 1795. It was designed in Doric style by James Wyatt, and the plans and the building work were pushed through by the Rev Samuel Hall, a curate at St Ann's Church, who became St Peter's first rector. The dome and clock were added in 1823. The church closed down in 1904, and was demolished in 1906. Interestingly, the four columns seen in our picture were taken to Knutsford to await use in another building, and that is where they are today - behind the King's Coffee House in King Street, Knutsford.

ST PETER'S CHURCH c1885 18302

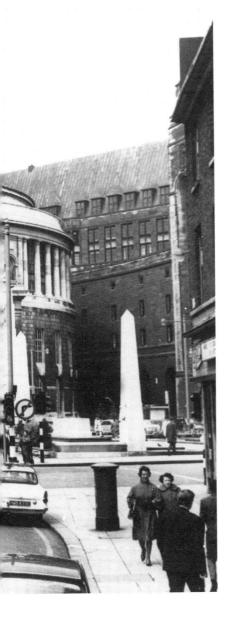

The Central Library and the Cenotaph dominate our photograph. The Central Library was opened by King George V in 1934, and it was then the largest public library in the country. The Cenotaph was built to a design by Sir Edwin Lutyens; it is similar to the one in Whitehall, and it stands where St Peter's Church once stood. There had been a large crypt in the church where over 2,500 of Manchester's citizens were laid to rest, because there was no graveyard. This was sealed and built over because of the problems of moving the collapsing coffins and skeletons. So when you stand on the platform to catch the tram, spare a thought for the 2,500 resting below.

ST PETER'S SQUARE

C1965 M21038

The Free Trade Hall we see here is the third building on this spot. When the subscription list opened for the cost of the building, it was referred to as the City Hall. Designed by Edward Walters, it was built between 1853-6 in a distinguished Victorian classical style. The arches around the veranda carry the shields of the Lancashire towns who supported the movement. The hall was gutted in the Second World War, and it took until November 1951 to reconstruct and re-open the hall.

THE FREE TRADE HALL c1885 18295

OWEN'S COLLEGE c1876 8295

The Manchester merchant John Owen, who died on 29 July 1846, made a fortune by hard work and honest dealing. After making sure that his relatives (he was a bachelor) were well provided for, he left the amazing sum of £100,000 in his will to form a college, where all faiths and denominations would be admitted. He believed very strongly in a full education for all religions. At first the college was on Quay Street, in central Manchester, but it soon outgrew the building. This is when the college we see in the photograph was planned.

This is the quadrangle of Owen's College, with the gateway out to Oxford Road on the right of the picture. In 1886-7 the Museum part of the college was among the buildings added to the complex. Owen's College was one of the first to hold classes for females (but not in mixed classes), and the first to have an engineering laboratory. In 1898, when parliament passed an Act for Manchester to have its own University, it was Owen's College which became the core of that University.

OWEN'S
COLLEGE 1891 29599

One of the founders of the Infirmary had been Dr White, and it was his son Charles who made many changes and advances in the treatment of women. He was the first doctor to specialise in 'female ailments'. He invented the sanitary towel, and advocated fresh air and hot water in the labour wards. The two statues guarding the hospital entrance are James Watt, right, and John Dalton, left. The Dalton statue was a bronze copy of the marble one by Chantry that stands in the town hall entrance. It was unveiled here on 26 July 1855, the third Dalton statue in Manchester. James Watt was to join him two years later on 26 June 1857. The James Watt statue is still there today, but the John Dalton one was moved; it now stands outside a University building in Chester Street.

THE INFIRMARY

1889 21893

THE INFIRMARY
1889   21892

THE ROYAL EXCHANGE
C1885 18261

Here we see the Royal Exchange from the corner of Market Street and Cross Street. This, the third Exchange, opened in October 1874; it had been built in two stages, so that members could move from the old to the new without disrupting things too much. The words around the great dome in the centre of the building were: 'A good name is rather to be chosen than great riches, and loving favour rather than silver and gold'. This building had Manchester's Telephone Exchange on the top floor - the posts carrying each line can be seen on the roof.

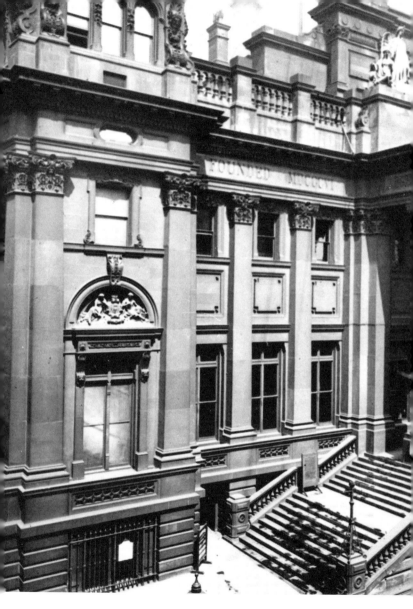

This lovely close-up view was taken from Cross Street. James Murgatroyd was the architect, and it was he who was invited back in April 1892 to oversee the taking down of the portico entrance and the bringing out of the front of the building to the pavement. Although the plans were carried out, there was a lot of disagreement over the payment for this extension; the Exchange had to form a limited company before the re-building could begin in August 1913. The First World War held up the work, and it was finally officially opened by King George V on 8 October 1921, nearly thirty years after the plans were first put forward. The Bolton firm of Bradshaw, Goss & Hope were the final architects.

THE ROYAL EXCHANGE
1889 21886

Hansom cabs wait on Oxford Road, Chorlton-on-Medlock. A horse bus has just passed them heading for the city centre; even a century ago, this was one of the main arteries into the town, just as it is today. The road starts at St Peter's Square, and is called Oxford Street until it crosses Whitworth Street, when it becomes Oxford Road. At one time, the houses on the street were rented and the money used to send boys to Oxford College, hence the name. Owen's College and the Whitworth Hall dominate our photograph.

OWEN'S COLLEGE

OXFORD ROAD 1895 36350

THE EYE HOSPITAL

1889   21911

If we look very closely, we can see that what we have here is actually three buildings. This complex included the Deaf and Dumb School, and Henshaw's Blind Asylum, complete with its own chapel. In 1810, Thomas Henshaw left £20,000 for the care of the blind, but the cost of the building had to be raised by public subscription, and it was 21 June 1837 before the building opened. At the time of our picture, Henshaw's had been going for almost fifty years, and had fostered about 1,000 blind persons. Henshaw's is still going today, and is doing great and much-needed work. In 1885 the Deaf and Dumb school had 36 boys and nearly 200 girls in residence. It was always a Children's School - an adult Deaf and Dumb Institute later opened at All Saints, Manchester.

THE BLIND ASYLUM C1885 18307

Manchester's Royal Jubilee Exhibition at Old Trafford opened on Tuesday, 2 May 1887. The Queen had declined the invitation to open this celebration of her 50 years on the throne, but Prince Edward agreed, and the Prince and Princess of Wales did the honours. The entrance they used was termed the Royal Entrance. The church tower is actually a replica of Manchester Cathedral; this was the centrepiece of an 'Old Manchester' exhibition, where a medieval Manchester was recreated.

THE ROYAL ENTRANCE, MANCHESTER EXHIBITION 1889 21901

A special railway station served the Exhibition. It had long platforms to accommodate the expected crowds, and plenty of staff on hand to help. They needed a large staff, as the number of visitors was massive. On one day over the Bank Holiday, a total of 74,600 visitors were recorded in one single day, and in the 166 days it was opened, 4.75 million people came to view the delights. The railway line was on the Manchester South Junction & Altrincham Railway, which had opened in 1849.

EXHIBITION STATION 1887 21904

MANCHESTER EXHIBITION

THE TOBOGGANING SLIDE 1887 21906

MANCHESTER
EXHIBITION FROM
TALBOT ROAD 1887 21902

This is a good close-up view of the main exhibition building that backed onto
Talbot Road, which got its name when Sir Humphry Trafford married Lady Annette
Talbot in 1823. You can see the 'fireproof' bridge which linked the two sites. The
designers and builders of the exhibition were Maxwell & Tuke, who went on to
design Blackpool Tower. Admission was one shilling (5p), except on a Friday, when
admission was 2s 6d. This was to give the upper classes a chance to visit without
mixing with too many working class people.

TRAFFORD PARK
1897 39049

Here we see the stand of the Lancashire Cricket Ground, called Old Trafford, as it looked just over a century ago. Fifty years earlier, the Manchester Cricket Club took over the Clifford cricket ground, situated between Chester Road and Talbot Road. The club had to move when the land was needed for the Art Treasure Exhibition, and it moved across the road to Old Trafford in 1857. The first game on this new ground was against the Liverpool Gentlemen, which Manchester won. In 1864 it was decided to form a County Club, and Lancashire County Cricket Club was born.

OLD TRAFFORD 1897 39050

This is a wonderfully patriotic photograph of the monument to Lancashire lad Sir Robert Peel, standing in the park named after him. The Manchester & Salford Parks Committee bought the Lark Hill Estate from William Garnett for £5,000 in 1845, who then gave them £500 back for their funds. It was this land which became Peel Park, and it was Robert Peel who supported the movement. The Park was opened on 22 August 1846, along with two other parks in Manchester, Queen's Park and Philip's Park. In 1850, Salford decided it wanted a tribute to Sir 'Bobbie' Peel, and the statue was unveiled on 8 May 1852, two years ahead of Manchester's tribute to Robert Peel. The cannons are trophies from the Crimean War sent in thanks for Salford's fund-raising.

SALFORD, PEEL PARK, PEEL STATUE 1889 22166

SALFORD, PEEL PARK
MUSEUM 1889 22164

The building seen here is properly called the Royal Free Museum &
Library; it opened on 9 January 1850, and was the first unconditionally
free municipal public library in the United Kingdom. The importance of this
event was marked by Queen Victoria and Prince Albert agreeing to become
Patrons, and the royal title was used up to 1940. Among its early visitors
were Queen Victoria, Prince Albert, the King of Portugal, the Duke of
Wellington, Mr Gladstone, John Ruskin, and many others.

SALFORD
THE ROYAL TECHNICAL INSTITUTE
1897   39043

The name Eccles comes from 'ecclesia', and means 'the place of the church', so it is no surprise that its central street is called Church Street. Our view is looking up from the Square towards the railway station. The square tower of St Mary's can be seen peeping out at the centre back of the picture. St Mary's is Eccles's parish church; it was mentioned in 1180, and is one of the very first founded in the area. Eccles Cross is on the very right of the picture in front of the District Bank.

ECCLES, CHURCH STREET
C1955 E88018

ECCLES, THE TOWN
HALL c1955 E88007

Up to 1974, Eccles was a town in its own right. It received its Charter of Incorporation in 1891, and then, of course, needed its own Town Hall. Here we see Eccles Town Hall in Church Street; at this time it was still its own master, but threatened with take-over even then by big brother Salford. The Town Hall was built in 1881 to a design by John Lowe with a pavilion roof and tall chimney pots. Just as striking is the Town Hall Tavern, black and white, next to it on the left.

Monton had been a separate village until the incorporation of Eccles, when it was taken under the new council's wing. Monton Green is also the name of the road in our photograph. Behind the photographer is the very large Broadoak Park, home of the Worsley Golf Club; the short road leading to the clubhouse is called Stableford Avenue. Like the other areas of Eccles and Salford, Monton likes to keep its own identity.

ECCLES, MONTON GREEN
c1955 E88029

99

We are in Liverpool Road. The bridge was built over the Bridgewater Canal in 1778, but it has been widened and strengthened many times since. The pubs on the corners of this cross-roads reflect the canal, with names like the Packet Boat, the Bridgewater, and the Navigation. Most of the buildings in this picture were swept away in the late 1960s and 1970s.

PATRICROFT

PATRICROFT BRIDGE
c1955 P158001

BARTON UPON IRWELL

BARTON BRIDGE ROAD c1955 B781025

This view shows the Barton Road Swing Bridge over the Manchester Ship Canal. Our photograph is taken from the Bridgewater Canal Aqueduct, which stands alongside this bridge. It used to be a source of frustration in the 1960s before the new Barton High Level Road Bridge (M60) was opened. Many motorists hurrying to work would find the bridge swung, and their way into Trafford Park held up, making them late for work.

GRAIN ELEVATORS
c1965 M21502

Here we have a fine aerial view of the large No 9 dock and the area around it. At the head of the dock can be seen the large No 2 grain elevator; later, this was so much trouble to pull down, that it took nearly three months before it was cleared away. There had been a No 1 grain elevator on Trafford Wharf, but this had been hit by an incendiary bomb during the Second World War, and after months of burning and smouldering because it was full of grain, was finally pulled down. No 8 dock is away to the right, and the area where the sheds are is now the Quay House.

This view shows the large expanse of water at the mouth of No 8 dock, which was the turning circle. It was here that the Manchester liners and Eleman boats could be turned round ready for their journey back out to sea. Though the official title of the docks was the Docks of the Manchester Ship Canal Company, they were mostly in Salford, with parts even in Stretford. The only part of the docks that were actually in Manchester was the top portion of No 1 dock Pomona.

THE SHIP
CANAL 1895 36387

THE SHIP CANAL

1895 36396

When the docks first opened, it took a while for them to reach their potential, but by 1900 they had started to show that they could be successful and profitable. Moves were then made to enlarge the dock, and the land belonging to the Manchester Racecourse Co was purchased ready to build No 9 dock. This dock, the largest of all the docks, was officially opened by King Edward VII and Queen Alexandra on a royal visit on 13 July 1905.

NO 9 DOCK
C1965 M21503

THE BARTON
AQUEDUCT
1894 33693

When the Duke of Bridgewater planned his canal into Manchester in 1760, the original plan was to stay on the Salford side of the Irwell. Because he could not purchase the land he wanted, he was forced to cross the River Irwell and go into Manchester via Stretford. He was given permission to skirt the Trafford Park Estate, but his big problem was crossing the Irwell, which he did with a beautiful stone aqueduct designed by James Brindley.

BARTON UPON IRWELL
THE SWING BRIDGES 1895 33691

This view shows the two bridges at Barton on Irwell both swung to let the paddle steamer 'Ivanhoe' pass. When the Ship Canal first opened (our view is only twelve months after that opening on 1 January 1894), many people wanted to travel, and see the wonders of this new waterway. A Ship Canal Pleasure Steamer Company was formed, and weekends and Bank Holidays would see two or three of these paddle steamers taking passengers on sight-seeing trips up and down the canal.

THE SHIP CANAL
c1965 M21505

INDEX

PLEASE HELP US BRING FRITH'S PHOTOGRAPHS TO LIFE

Our authors do their best to recount the history of the places they write about. They give insights into how particular towns and villages developed, they describe the architecture of streets and buildings, and they discuss the lives of famous people who lived there. But however knowledgeable our authors are, the story they tell is necessarily incomplete.

Frith's photographs are so much more than plain historical documents. They are living proofs of the flow of human life down the generations. They show real people at real moments in history; and each of those people is the son or daughter of someone, the brother or sister, aunt or uncle, grandfather or grandmother of someone else. All of them lived, worked and played in the streets depicted in Frith's photographs.

We would be grateful if you would tell us about the many places shown in our photographs—the streets with their buildings, shops, businesses and industries. Describe your own memories of life in those streets: what it was like growing up there, who ran the local shop and what shopping was like years ago; if your workplace is shown tell us about your working day and what the building is used for now. With your help more and more Frith photographs can be brought to life, and vital memories preserved for posterity.

We will gradually add your comments and stories to the archive for the benefit of historians of the future. Wherever possible, we will try to include some of your comments in future editions of our books. Moreover, if you spot errors in dates, titles or other facts, please let us know, because our archive records are not always completely accurate—they rely on 150 years of human endeavour and hand-compiled records.

So please write, fax or email us with your stories and memories. Thank you!

CHOOSE ANY PHOTOGRAPH FROM THIS BOOK

for your FREE Mounted Print. Order further prints at half price

Fill in and cut out the voucher on the next page and return it with your remittance for £2.50 for postage, packing and handling to UK addresses (US $5.00 for USA and Canada). For all other overseas addresses include £5.00 post and handling.
Choose any photograph included in this book. Make sure you quote its unique reference number eg. 42365 (it is mentioned after the photograph date. 1890 / 42365). Your SEPIA print will be approx 12" x 8" and mounted in a cream mount with a burgundy rule line (overall size 14" x 11").

Mounted Print
Overall size 14 x 11 inches

Order additional Mounted Prints at HALF PRICE - If you would like to order more Frith prints from this book, possibly as gifts for friends and family, you can buy them at half price (with no extra postage and handling costs) - only £7.49 each (UK orders), US $14.99 each (USA and Canada).

* IMPORTANT!

These special prices are only available if you order at the same time as you order your free mounted print. You must use the ORIGINAL VOUCHER on the facing page (no copies permitted). We can only despatch to one address.

Have your Mounted Prints framed (UK orders only) - For an extra £14.95 per print you can have your mounted print(s) framed in an elegant polished wood and gilt moulding, overall size 16" x 13" (no additional postage).

FRITH PRODUCTS AND SERVICES

All Frith photographs are available for you to buy as framed or mounted prints. From time to time, other illustrated items such as Address Books, Calendars, Table Mats are also available. Already, almost 50,000 Frith archive photographs can be viewed and purchased on the internet through the Frith website.

For more detailed information on Frith companies and products, visit:

www.francisfrith.co.uk

For further information, trade, or author enquiries, contact:

The Francis Frith Collection, Frith's Barn, Teffont, Salisbury SP3 5QP

Tel: +44 (0) 1722 716 376 Fax: +44 (0) 1722 716 881 Email: sales@francisfrith.co.uk

Voucher

*for FREE
and Reduced Price
Frith Prints*

*Do not photocopy this voucher. Only the original is valid, so please fill it in,
cut it out and return it to us with your order.*

	Picture ref no	Page number	Qty	Mounted @ £7.49 UK @$14.99 US	Framed + £14.95 (UK only)	US orders Total $	UK orders Total £
1			1	Free of charge*	£	$	£
2				£7.49 ($14.99)	£	$	£
3				£7.49 ($14.99)	£	$	£
4				£7.49 ($14.99)	£	$	£
5				£7.49 ($14.99)	£	$	£
6				£7.49 ($14.99)	£	$	£

*Please allow 28 days
for delivery*

	* Post & handling	$5.00	£2.50
	Total Order Cost	US $	£

Title of this book . . . .

I enclose a cheque / postal order (UK) for £ . . . . $ . . . .
payable to 'Francis Frith Collection' (USA orders 'Frith USA Inc')

OR debit my Mastercard / Visa / Switch (UK) / Amex card / Discover (USA)
(credit cards only on non UK and US orders), card details below

Card Number

Issue No (Switch only)   Valid from (Amex/Switch)

Expires   Signature

Name Mr/Mrs/Ms . . . .

Address . . . .

. . . .

. . . .

Postcode/Zip. . . . . Country . . . .

Daytime Tel No . . . .   Valid to 31/12/06

PAYMENT CURRENCY: We only accept payment in £ Sterling or US $.
If you are ordering **from any other country, please pay by credit card,**
and you will be charged in one of these currencies.